CLOSE YET APART

A SIMPLE GUIDE TO UNDERSTANDING AVOIDANT ATTACHMENT

VALERIE GRAY

ST. JAMES PRESS

For Tiffany and Grant

CONTENTS

INTRODUCTION

The Nature of Attachment

Few factors are as strong and widespread in the human experience as attachment. It is a natural want, a pull that ties us to others and grounds us in the turbulent sea of human emotions and experiences. Our behaviors, convictions, and even our very identities are shaped by this powerful force, which also influences the fabric of our existence.

In its purest form, attachment is our emotional connection to people. It begins the minute we are born, influencing our connections with our primary caregivers and establishing the framework for our relationships with other people throughout our lives. These early connections (or lack thereof) seep into the very fiber of our being and have a profound impact on a variety of decisions, actions, and emotions.

Exploring the depths of the psyche, home to our deepest fears, hopes, and wants, is necessary to understand the nature of attachment. These ties serve as our safety nets and anchors that keep us connected to a sense of security and belonging. However, they can also act as our chains, holding us captive to habits that may not be in our best interests.

But before we can truly understand the depth and scope of attachment's influence, we must first get familiar with its many manifestations, or what psychologists call "attachment styles." This brings us to a basic summary of these types, each reflecting a different manner of interacting with and engaging with others.

A Brief Overview: Attachment Styles

According to attachment theory, which is based on the ground-breaking research of John Bowlby, our early interactions with caregivers impact how we relate to others as adults. *Secure, Anxious, Avoidant,* and *Disorganized* attachment styles are the four main ones that result from this. Each provides a unique view of relational dynamics and a road map for comprehending how we connect and form bonds.

The Secure attachment style, frequently regarded as the gold standard, is distinguished by a balanced perspective on interpersonal interactions. These people find it quite simple to develop strong ties, give assistance, and ask for it when needed. Their interactions are typically stable, characterized by respect and understanding between them.

The Anxious style, in comparison, has a hint of abandonment anxiety. People with this type desire intimacy and are frequently focused on their relationships. They could appear "clingy," continually looking to their spouses for approval and comfort. The

Avoidant style is at the other extreme of the spectrum. People in this place passionately defend their autonomy, frequently at the expense of emotional connection. They may avoid intimacy for fear of becoming vulnerable or losing their independence.

The fourth, Disorganized attachment, is a little more difficult to understand and is frequently brought on by trauma or erratic caregiving. Relationships with these people can be turbulent and unexpected because of the confused mixture of nervous and avoidant behaviors they frequently exhibit.

Understanding the Importance of Attachment in Our Lives

Not only a psychological idea, but attachment is also a vital force. The influence of attachment styles permeates everything we do, from the relationships we build to the partners we pick. Our interpersonal outlook, how we handle disagreement, and how much trust we invest in other people can all be influenced by our attachment type.

Our attachment type can affect aspects of our lives beyond our intimate relationships. Those early habits set in our childhood can have an impact on our career decisions, friendships, and even our sense of self-worth. For instance, a person who is avoidantly attached could avoid teamwork and prefer solo initiatives, whereas a person who is anxiously attached might continually seek approval from superiors.

Furthermore, our attachment patterns are entangled with our overall physical and mental health. The effects of our attachment style are felt in every area of life, from stress levels to general contentment. This might be the first step toward self-improvement and richer, more meaningful friendships if you recognize and understand it.

What This Book Aims to Achieve

This work is fundamentally a beacon, shedding light on the frequently misunderstood territory of avoidant attachment. We seek to debunk the myths around this special mode of relating and connecting through synthesizing scientific discoveries, true stories, and professional viewpoints.

This goes beyond a purely theoretical investigation. Instead, it is a helpful manual that gives persons who identify with avoidant attachment and others who want to learn more about it tools, tactics, and insights. An in-depth examination of this attachment style's origins is done to promote comprehension, empathy, and personal development.

This investigation also touches on societal, cultural, and more general psychological issues, going beyond the individual. The aim is to provide readers with a comprehensive understanding that will enable them to go through their relationships and personal journeys with more awareness and intention.

The Effects of Attachment on Relationships, Careers, and Self-Value

Our attachment style is individual and shapes how we see the world; it's like a fingerprint on the glass of our existence. The most obvious settings for these habits to manifest themselves are in relationships, both romantic and platonic. Our attachment inclinations choreograph the dance of intimacy and distance, trust and mistrust, vulnerability and defense.

However, it has an impact beyond interpersonal ties. Our attachment style can influence how we work, collaborate, and even where we go in our careers. An avoidantly attached person could choose roles with autonomy and have difficulty working in a team or under strict supervision.

Furthermore, our attachment behaviors and our sense of self-worth are closely related. These early relationship blueprints can be linked to how we view ourselves, our conviction that we deserve love and connection, and our overall sense of value.

Common Misconceptions about Avoidant Attachment

The concept of avoidant attachment is clouded with myths and misconceptions, much like any other intricate psychological topic. Some people who avoid getting involved are characterized as "cold" or "emotionless," while others may write them off as commitment avoiders. These superficial descriptions do avoidant attachment a disservice by failing to convey its complexity and depth.

Far from being absent of emotion, avoidant attachment frequently results from a deep-seated dread of vulnerability. These people may have grown up learning that being too close might hurt, so they now keep their distance to protect themselves. Contrary to popular assumption, they also desire connection, but they go about it cautiously and for their own benefit.

It's imperative to dispel these myths to gain a deeper understanding, promote empathy, and mend relational divides.

The Underlying Neuroscience

Recent developments in neuroscience have provided new insight into how the brain processes attachment patterns. According to brain imaging studies, our attachment preferences may be correlated with the activation and operation of specific brain regions, particularly those related to stress, reward, and social bonding.

Stimuli that could cause sensations of vulnerability or intimacy can cause avoidantly attached people to experience stress by activating their brain's stress pathways. It seems as though the brain reacts defensively when emotional connection is perceived as a potential threat. This neurological understanding provides a more empathetic perspective by highlighting that these reactions are frequently ingrained and habitual.

Relationship to Individual Histories and Upbringing

In many respects, our attachment patterns reflect our past. Our relational blueprints are significantly shaped by our early experiences, particularly those with our primary caregivers. Secure attachment can be fostered through consistent, compassionate care, but other attachment styles might develop due to inconsistency, neglect, or trauma.

Many people who have avoidant attachment may be able to recall times in their past when being vulnerable was frowned upon or when independence was the only option to guarantee emotional security. Understanding how the past and present are related is essential since it opens doors to healing and development.

Real-world Examples: Avoidant Attachment Case Studies

The theoretical frameworks are given life in this book through real-world narratives. These emotionally and experientially rich tales provide a window into the world of avoidant attachment. These experiences highlight the humanity behind the psychiatric jargon, from stories of love and sorrow to quests for self-discovery.

We hope to promote empathy, compassion, and a feeling of the commonality of the human experience by sharing these experiences. They serve as a reminder that every action, every coping technique, conceals a deeper story, a person, and a yearning for connection.

How You Can Benefit from This Book

This book promises insights and revelations whether you identify with avoidant attachment, are in a relationship with someone who does or is just curious soul. It's not just about comprehension; it's also about development, empowerment, and creating stronger relationships.

You'll be given the tools, techniques, and professional insights to navigate your relationships with increased awareness. Additionally, you'll have a deeper awareness of your own path and the complex dance of human connections by understanding the wider significance of attachment patterns.

ONE
THE ORIGINS OF AVOIDANT ATTACHMENT

Birth of Attachment Theory

In the middle of the 20th century, the ever-evolving field of psychology stumbled across the revolutionary concept of attachment theory. According to the hypothesis, people are wired to want to create strong emotional connections with specific individuals. These connections, rooted in our evolutionary past, act as anchors and give us a safe haven from which to explore the rest of the world.

The survival concept lies at the heart of attachment theory. Early humans required carers to protect them from hazards during the delicate stages of infancy and childhood. Emotional attachments were created as a result of this intrinsic want to be near a guardian. These connections have evolved over time to affect not only our survival but also our mental health and social interactions.

The universality of attachment theory is what makes it so

brilliant. Regardless of a person's culture, upbringing, or past, they have a fundamental desire for stable bonding. It serves as the foundation around which all of our other interactions and relationships are created, directing our actions, expectations, and reactions to other people.

Early Observations in Children

Children's behavior, especially when separated from their primary caregivers, provided early clues for attachment theory. These separations, whether in hospitals, orphanages, or during evacuations during a war, had a significant psychological impact. Many of these kids showed signs of hopelessness and indifference, as well as a strong desire for connection and social contact.

These observations had a significant impact on John Bowlby, who is considered one of the founding fathers of attachment theory. According to his theory, these behaviors weren't random occurrences but rather physiologically planned reactions intended to keep the caregiver nearby. All of the crying, clinging, and eventually despair were adaptive behaviors meant to engender care and safety.

The detailed investigations and tests that would come later were made possible by these initial observations. They emphasized the value of the caregiver-child link and how damage to it may affect a child's emotional and psychological health.

Bowlby and Ainsworth: Pioneers in the Field

Although John Bowlby's work on attachment theory was innovative, it was his partnership with Mary Ainsworth that brought the concept to the forefront of psychology. Bowlby laid the theoretical foundation, and Ainsworth supported it with rigorous study and observations.

The research done by Ainsworth in Baltimore and later in Uganda yielded priceless insights into the dynamics of the caregiver-infant interaction.

Based on how babies reacted to their carers and how caregivers reacted to their babies, she identified unique types of attachment. The seeds of secure, anxious, and avoidant attachment types were sown in this dynamic interplay.

Their joint efforts connected theoretical ideas with empirical behaviors to provide a comprehensive picture of attachment. The synthesis of Bowlby's theories and Ainsworth's research techniques led to a paradigm change in our understanding of child development, parenting, and interpersonal interactions.

The Strange Situation Experiment

An important turning point in attachment research was Ainsworth's "Strange Situation" experiment, which was carried out in the late 1960s. The purpose of this structured observational study was to examine the characteristics of baby attachment behaviors. In a controlled environment, a mother and her infant experience brief separations and reunions.

When observing the infant's responses to these split-second

separations and reunions, observers classified their actions into various attachment styles. Secure, anxious-resistant (or ambivalent), and anxious-avoidant were the three main styles found. Infants who were avoidantly attached exhibited a certain set of behaviors. They appeared nonchalant or apathetic during the separations. On a more subtle level, however, physiological reactions showed increased distress. Avoidant attachment was defined by the contrast between their outward actions and inward state.

The "Strange Situation" established Bowlby's attachment theory and the premise that our early interactions with caregivers have a significant impact on how we approach relationships throughout our lives.

Characteristics of Avoidantly Attached Infants

Infants who are avoidantly attached have a distinct set of behaviors. They might appear independent at first glance, rarely sobbing or displaying overt signs of grief when taken away from their caregivers. This apparent independence, nevertheless, hides an underlying inner volatility.

According to research, even though these children may not clearly express a need for comfort, their physiological reactions, such as elevated heart rates or cortisol levels, reveal otherwise. It seems they've learned to hide their outward signs of need or discomfort, perhaps due to previous emotions being ignored or inconsistently met.

Their manner upon reunion is yet another unique quality. Infants who are avoidantly attached may actively avoid or disregard their caregiver, unlike securely attached infants who seek comfort and contact. This behavior is considered a defensive tactic meant to reduce the likelihood of rejection or disappointment.

These early patterns are crucial because they frequently lay the groundwork for how these kids will negotiate relationships in the future and shape their perceptions of intimacy, vulnerability, and trust.

How Parenting Styles Contribute

The child's temperament and the caregiver's actions both have an impact on the attachment dance; it is a two-way street. A child's attachment style is significantly influenced by parental behaviors, which can range from being responsive and attentive to being dismissive and inconsistent.

Researchers have noted that parents who constantly oppose overt displays of emotion or vulnerability in avoidant attachment may unintentionally encourage this tendency in their kids. Youngsters may learn to repress their screams, needs, or feelings if they observe that they are either disregarded or met with discomfort.

But parenting isn't about being flawless. It's all about reliability, kinship, and response. Knowing how one's parenting style affects attachment can serve as a mirror and a window at the same time, reflecting current dynamics and presenting opportunities for change and development.

Cultural Perspectives on Avoidance

The fundamental ideas of attachment theory are universal, but how they are expressed varies among cultures. Some cultures place a strong priority on self-reliance, emotional control, and independence. In certain settings, avoidant attachment-related behaviors may not only be prevalent but also praised and rewarded.

For instance, emotional restraint is regarded as a virtue and a sign of maturity and self-control in some Eastern cultures. On the other hand, some Western cultures may place a strong emphasis on uniqueness and independence from a young age, discreetly discouraging overly dependent behavior or overt emotional expression.

It's crucial to understand these cultural quirks. By providing additional levels of understanding, we ensure that attachment types aren't assessed in isolation but in the context of a wider range of societal values, expectations, and conventions.

Avoidance Across Different Societies

Illuminating insights can be gained by delving more deeply into the parenting customs of different nations. For instance, encouraging baby freedom, including having them sleep outside in safe locations, is typical in some Nordic nations. In contrast, co-sleeping is commonplace in many Asian communities, which value close physical proximity.

Physical closeness does not necessarily translate into emotional connection, though. While physical intimacy may be favored in some communities, emotional expression may be discouraged. Conversely, open emotional communication may be encouraged in civilizations that value physical independence.

Diverse expressions of attachment styles, including avoidance, are seen throughout different societies due to this complicated interaction between societal norms, parental techniques, and individual temperaments.

The Genetics of Attachment: Nature vs. Nurture

When researching the causes of avoidant attachment, the age-old question of nature vs. nurture always comes up. Do our attachment patterns simply result from our environment, or are they physically predisposed?

Despite early proponents' strong environmental bias, new genetic and neurological discoveries point to a more nuanced picture. An individual's attachment style may be influenced by certain genetic markers that predispose them to greater sensitivity or reactivity.

However, genes do not determine fate. The environment, especially early caregiving experiences, shapes how these genetic predispositions manifest; they serve as a template. In essence, the dance between our genetic makeup and our early relational experiences determines our attachment pattern.

What Are the Evolutionary Benefits of Avoidant Attachment?

Every characteristic or habit that has survived the evolutionary process probably has some advantages. Even though it seems illogical, avoidant attachment is no exception.

Emotional self-reliance is advantageous in situations where receiving constant care is uncertain or where being vulnerable might be seen as a weakness. An avoidantly attached person reduces the chance of rejection or disappointment by not expressing their need or suffering externally.

Additionally, avoidant actions might be advantageous in civilizations with limited resources or when survival depends on self-sufficiency. One survives unforeseen circumstances by learning to depend less on others and more on oneself.

The difficulties of avoidant attachment, however, become increasingly obvious in contemporary, networked societies where emotional relationships and partnerships are vital, opening the door for investigation, insight, and possible progress.

TWO
RECOGNIZING AVOIDANT BEHAVIOR IN ADULTS

The Fear of Intimacy

The doorway to a universe of shared emotions, frailties, and experiences is intimacy. Most people rely on it as the cornerstone of meaningful relationships. However, some people pause or even retreat as they approach this gateway's threshold. What is this terror that holds them captive?

For those who are avoidantly attached, closeness is a dangerous place. Each step taken to establish a closer bond brings back painful memories of betrayals or abandonments from the past. The very act of baring one's soul, central to intimacy, becomes an act fraught with danger. Intimacy is a possible source of pain rather than the promise of happiness and understanding.

We learn more and more that this anxiety isn't just a whim or caprice. It is a protective system developed through many years, if not decades, of experience. It is a shield, but one with two edges. It shields children from potential harm, but it also keeps them apart from real connections.

Also, this isn't a static situation. The avoidantly attached person changes, adapts, and occasionally, with compassion and encouragement, even learns to let down their guard. Although the journey is difficult, it is attainable with self-awareness.

Push-Pull Dynamics in Relationships

Imagine participating in a dance where you are pushed away one second and drawn closer the next. The push-pull dynamics in relationships with avoidant people are characterized by this pattern, which is frequently puzzling and emotionally taxing.

Early in a relationship, it may feel intense, passionate, and even consuming. Like everyone else, the avoidant person yearns for love and connection. But when the connection grows stronger, the idea of a deeper emotional connection seems intimidating. The pushing starts.

The receiving partner frequently struggles with a storm of feelings. confusion, suffering, and even wrath. "Why this sudden change?" they ponder. What happened? However, what they frequently miss is that this interaction is more about the avoidant person's mental turmoil and less about them.

Understanding its roots and patterns is the first step to navigating the dynamic, which can be difficult.

There's More to Emotional Inaccessibility Than "Being Closed Off"

In conversations about relationships, the phrase "emotionally unavailable" is commonly used. However, it's not simply about being "closed off." When you explore further, it's like removing the layers of an onion; each one reveals a different aspect of the avoidant person's emotional environment.

First off, this lack of availability isn't a decision. It's not about playing the field or acting distant just for effect. It is fundamentally a defense mechanism that was developed as a result of painful prior events where emotional vulnerability was encountered.

There is a tornado of repressed feelings, wants, and memories hidden below the façade of detachedness. memories of times when they tried to reach out but were rejected. a need for real connection that may have never been expressed.

For them, maintaining balance is a delicate task. They are split between the want to connect and the crippling fear that it might do them harm once more. Understanding and patience become the keys to removing these emotional barriers, as with other avoidance-related behaviors.

Independence or Isolation?

The independent person is frequently portrayed as powerful, independent, and capable of standing alone. But at what point does independence become isolation?

The line is frequently hazy for those who are avoidantly attached. They are fiercely independent because they firmly believe they cannot rely on others. In their view, relying on someone is a recipe for disappointment or heartache.

However, there is frequently a secret yearning hidden beneath this appearance of independence. a longing for intimacy, for exchanging experiences, and for the comfort of company. The irony is obvious. They frequently end up in the cold corridors of isolation because of their own defense mechanism, which promises to protect them.

Understanding this paradox is essential for the avoidant person as well as any possible partners. Only then can the journey from isolation back to genuine independence commence.

Defining Personal Space: Setting Boundaries or Pushing Away?

Every person has boundaries, invisible lines that define their emotional and physical personal space. These boundaries, however, frequently take on a distinct tone in the context of avoidant attachment.

They transform into towering, frequently impregnable barriers rather than flexible lines. Setting boundaries may appear to be a straightforward action, but doing it frequently amounts to pushing someone away and is a sign of vulnerability anxiety.

Making a distinction between the two is crucial. Boundaries are beneficial and essential. They protect us and are a reflection of our self-respect. But these limits stop being helpful to us when they turn into barriers.

The challenge for those caught in the web of avoidant

attachment is to identify these obstacles and, with time and assistance, learn to overcome them.

Commitment Issues Explained

In a relationship, the word "commitment" connotes a pledge. a commitment to time, allegiance, and shared futures. But for many people with avoidant attachment patterns, commitment feels constrictive, like chains that bind them.

The process of thought is interesting. An intertwining of life and dependency is implied by commitment. Additionally, reliance is a surefire way to wind up upset or disappointed. Thus, the avoidant person shies away, fearing the very bond they often deeply crave.

The cycle is painful as well as illuminating. A relationship's early phases may be intense, even heady. However, the barriers rise as the relationship progresses toward a more serious commitment. The retreat begins.

Understanding this perspective sheds light on why some avoidantly attached individuals might shy away from long-term commitments or become restless in established relationships, always looking for an exit.

Serial Dating and the Fear of Settling Down

New beginnings and fresh starts have a universal charm. However, for those who have avoidant tendencies, this allure frequently turns into a cycle—a serial dating cycle.

Every new connection provides the excitement of the hunt and the joy of discovery without placing demands on a deeper level of emotional commitment. The surface is intriguing and unintimidating. But when the connection necessitates greater depth and openness, the old worries surface. Usually, the end comes quickly.

The fear of commitment is not the only factor in this trend. It also concerns a darker, more primal fear: the fear of vulnerability, of being truly seen and known. And perhaps, being found wanting.

Yet, hope springs eternal. This pattern can be identified and, with time, even changed with knowledge and assistance.

Passive-Aggressive Behavior and Avoidance

Open conflict is difficult for most people. But it's a dangerous place for those who shun it. let's talk about passive-aggressive behavior.

Sarcasm, neglect, and subtly provocative language are examples of indirect expression instead of direct communication. It could appear less confronting at first glance, even innocent. But its undercurrents have the potential to undermine a relationship.

It is crucial to understand where this habit came from. It's not necessary to be challenging. It involves expressing unhappiness, anxiety, or wrath without exposing oneself to vulnerability or direct conflict.

Yet, like all patterns, it can be transformed. The first step? Recognizing it for what it is — a defense mechanism, not a character flaw.

The Myth of the "Lone Wolf"

The "Lone Wolf" is unattached to society, alone, and independent. Many people, especially those with avoidant tendencies, can relate to this image. It is, however, a myth and a glorified representation of seclusion.

There is a truth hidden beneath the charm of this figure. Humans are sociable beings by nature. Even those of us who are the most isolated want belonging, connection, and company.

The "Lone Wolf" persona is a barrier and confinement for those who choose to avoid attachment. It confines them in a world of loneliness while also validating their isolationist conduct.

A balanced approach is the way forward. acknowledging and nourishing the fundamental human urge for connection while simultaneously embracing one's need for isolation. It's a journey, but one that's worthwhile taking.

ONE TRUTH EMERGES from the confusing world of adult avoidant conduct: every pattern and every behavior has a backstory and a history. The first step toward more fulfilling relationships, healing, and fulfillment is realizing and understanding these patterns.

THREE
THE WORLD THROUGH AVOIDANT EYES

How Avoidantly Attached Individuals View Love

For many, love is a cozy embrace that makes them feel at home. But love frequently takes on a different face for people with avoidant attachment. They view love as erratic, irrational, and even treacherous. The deeper they dive into it, the more uncertain the waters become.

Every act of love, every gesture, is dissected and examined for dangers or pitfalls. It's not cynicism per se; rather, it's a protective instinct, a wall against potential harm. Although they may long for the recklessness that love promises, they are constantly cautious of its depths.

The irony is obvious. While they, like all of us, long for the warmth and closeness of love, their internal stories and prior experiences frequently skew their perceptions. They are caught in a dance — drawn to love, yet wary of its embrace.

Their relationships often bear the brunt of this dance. Partners may sense the distant, even icy demeanor without recognizing the emotional tumult happening inside. Awareness of this paradox is the first step towards developing a stronger connection.

Trust Problems and Their Causes

The basis of any relationship is trust. But for those who eschew attachment, trust is a difficult thing to come by. Every approach and every assurance are met with a dash of mistrust. A history of unfulfilled promises, betrayals, or disappointments lies at the root of this skepticism.

These trust problems didn't just appear suddenly. They represent the result of years, and perhaps decades, of experiences. Moments when they tried to reach out but were rejected or disappointed. These incidents eventually combine to form a story: the world isn't reliable.

It's not a static state, though. These trust obstacles can be overcome with understanding, persistence, and frequently therapeutic interventions. The path is difficult but doable, leading to a place where trust is not the exception but the rule.

Perceived Threats: Real vs. Imagined

Distinguishing actual and imagined risks is frequently necessary when viewing the world via the avoidant attachment lens. A casual comment from a spouse or a friend that isn't returned might escalate into perceived slights or betrayals.

These impressions are not arbitrary. They have a strong feeling of self-preservation at their core. The avoidant person constantly scans the horizon for prospective risks and frequently sees them where none exist.

This continual watchfulness might become exhausting. They are deprived of the pleasure of impromptu interactions and of taking others at their word. Every interaction turns into a potential minefield, and each gesture could be dangerous.

But, as with most habits, becoming aware of them is the first step toward change. Creating a road to more sincere and satisfying friendships is possible by identifying and differentiating these imagined threats from the actual ones.

The Role of Past Traumas

The avoidantly attached frequently have severe psychological scars from prior tragedies. These traumas, whether blatant betrayals or subtle neglects, shape their worldview, coloring their perceptions and interactions.

It's important to realize that not all of these experiences are dramatic. It can occasionally result from subtle, persistent invalidation experienced during childhood, the sensation of being ignored, or the lack of a secure emotional environment. These instances, which are frequently overlooked or hidden, are crucial in forming the avoidant narrative.

Here, therapy plays a significant role in locating and exposing these traumas. It is a path toward acceptance, understanding, and, finally, healing. The avoidant person can discriminate between previous traumas and current reality along this trip, allowing them to free themselves from their bonds.

Avoiding Vulnerability at All Costs

For many people, being vulnerable opens the door to meaningful friendships. But for those who shun attachment, vulnerability is a dangerous place. Exposing one's scars and baring one's soul can be a form of self-destructive behavior.

This fear of weakness is a defensive mechanism. Moments of vulnerability in the past might have been treated with mockery, disregard, or even treachery. Over time, it becomes evident that the message is vulnerability leads to suffering.

The richness of life, however, frequently necessitates vulnerability. Whether in interpersonal interactions, creative expression, or reflective moments. They lose out on deeper connections and self-awareness by avoiding it.

Self-sufficiency as a Defense Mechanism

The idea of self-sufficiency is frequently romanticized as characterizing someone who is independent and stands tall. This self-sufficiency, however, frequently serves a dual purpose for the avoidantly attached; it acts as both a strength and a defense.

Dependence suggests fragility and a blurring of lines. And for those who are avoidantly linked, this blurring frequently brings back regrets or recollections of betrayals from the past. As a result, they construct a fortress of independence, ensuring they never have to depend on anyone.

Although their independence benefits them in many areas, it also isolates them. Relationships, after all, rely on shared vulnerability and mutual dependency.

Recognizing this defense mechanism, and understanding its

roots, is the first step toward building bridges. Bridges that allow them to be self-sufficient yet connected.

The Fear of Being "Needy"

The adjective "needy" frequently connotes a negative trait. It conveys a sense of dependency and stress. This anxiety over being viewed as "needy" is virtually paralyzing for those who resist being attached.

Behind this fear lies a deep-seated belief — needs make one vulnerable, and vulnerability leads to pain. This belief often manifests in relationships where they might suppress their desires, and their needs, presenting a façade of independence.

However, there is a need for understanding, connection, and love at the core of every human encounter. Denying these needs just suppresses them rather than negating them.

The journey, then, is one of acceptance. Accepting that having needs isn't a sign of weakness but a testament to our shared humanity.

Attachment and Career Choices

Avoidant attachment behaviors are not just found in intimate partnerships. They frequently impact career decisions, work relationships, and professional choices.

People who are avoidantly attached could be drawn to occupations that require little connection with others so they can keep their boundaries unchallenged. They frequently perform well in jobs that require independence, control, and accuracy.

However, every profession necessitates some degree of

interpersonal contact, teamwork, or reliance. The avoidant habits may manifest in certain situations, potentially impeding career advancement.

It's crucial to understand these patterns and spot how they appear in the workplace. It opens the door to more satisfying employment options and wholesome professional connections.

The Avoidant Inner Monologue

Every avoidantly attached person has an interior monologue, a constant stream of ideas, convictions, and narratives hidden beneath their outward appearance. As it directs their interactions and constricts their experiences, this monologue frequently acts as both a compass and a prison.

Past events, perceived slights, and ingrained views are all mixed together in this story. It frequently strengthens their propensity to avoid situations by validating their worries and anxieties.

But it may be changed, just like any story. This monologue can be changed via self-reflection, counseling, and deliberate effort. A story that is more liberating and empowering could develop, opening the door to more sincere interactions and encounters.

Avoidant Attachment and Mental Health

Avoidant attachment and mental health are intricately linked. While avoidant behaviors in themselves aren't pathological, they can sometimes exacerbate or intersect with mental health challenges.

In those with avoidant tendencies, anxiety, depression, or other mental health illnesses may manifest differently. Their attachment type may be visible in their coping techniques, interactions, and therapeutic journeys.

For therapists, partners, and even the avoidantly attached persons themselves, understanding this interaction is essential. Individualized therapy approaches, patient comprehension, and self-awareness can achieve holistic mental well-being.

FOUR
THE IMPACT ON RELATIONSHIPS

The Avoidant and Anxious Combo: A Volatile Mix

Enter the dance of attachment styles: the avoidant, who values distance, and the anxious, who craves closeness. When they are in a relationship, it's like fire meets gasoline. The worried partner's desire for ongoing reassurance frequently clashes with the avoidant's desire for space and independence.

In their search for connection, the anxious person may accidentally drive their avoidant spouse further away. They crave validation, regular contact, and presence to alleviate their feelings of abandonment and rejection.

The avoidant person, on the other hand, retreats deeper into their shell as they are overwhelmed by this imagined barrage of neediness. Their distancing strategies — delayed reactions, evasiveness, and emotional unavailability — increase their partner's concerns.

This pairing has the potential to become a self-fulfilling

prophecy in many ways. The very worries and insecurities both partners seek to avoid become prominent in their relationship. Pursuit and retreat patterns emerge, leading to increasing instability.

However, there is room for development within this tumultuous environment. Both partners can realize their habits and disrupt the repetitive dance of push and pull through awareness, understanding, and therapeutic action. However, it necessitates effort, patience, and a willingness to tackle deep-seated concerns.

How Avoidance Affects Long-Term Relationships

Intimacy, trust, and constancy are essential in long-term relationships. However, the characteristics of avoidant attachment – the dread of closeness, distrust, and unpredictability – can strain these bonds. Over time, the partner of an avoidantly attached person may feel as though they are in a relationship that's a mirage: there yet distant.

This distance isn't always physical. It emerges as an emotional retreat, withdrawal during confrontations, or an unexplainable coolness, even during personal moments. This can weaken the foundations of a relationship over time.

However, it is critical to understand that this behavior is not motivated by contempt or a lack of affection. It's a defensive mechanism developed over time that has taught the avoidant individual to shield their heart.

In such relationships, the process involves patience and gradually gaining trust. It's about providing safe environments where people can disclose their vulnerabilities without fear and where closeness doesn't mean entrapment.

This trip, however, is not one-sided. The avoidant spouse must also acknowledge their tendencies and understand the consequences of their behavior on the relationship. Through mutual effort, long-term relationships can navigate the maze of avoidance, emerging stronger.

The Role of Avoidance in Friendships

While romantic relationships are frequently the victims of avoidant behavior, friendships are not exempt. The dynamics may change, but the patterns do not. An avoidant person may have many acquaintances but few 'close pals.'

Friendship necessitates openness, the sharing of personal stories, anxieties, and joys. This can be difficult terrain for the avoidantly attached. They may avoid difficult conversations, keep a cheery demeanor, and avoid circumstances that require an emotional connection.

While this strategy protects adolescents against potential harm, it also deprives them of the joys of deep, fulfilling connections. Friends may regard them as aloof, distant, or even uncaring over time.

However, chances for advancement exist within these patterns. Friendships, because they are free of romantic pressures, can sometimes serve as safe havens for the avoidantly attached to explore their weaknesses. They can be the testing grounds, where they learn to lower their guards gradually.

However, it necessitates recognizing their habits, understanding their worries, and having the patience to traverse them.

Avoidant people can cultivate strong and lasting connections with effort.

Parenting with Avoidant Attachment

Parenting, with all of its challenges and demands, can be especially difficult for individuals who are avoidant. Parenting necessitates vulnerability, ongoing availability, and a high level of emotional connection.

These obligations may be difficult for the avoidant parent. They may be extraordinary in terms of meeting their child's bodily requirements, as well as guaranteeing his or her safety, education, and well-being. They may, however, falter when it comes to emotional availability.

It's a difficult dance. On the one hand, the child's need for proximity may exacerbate the parent's dread of engulfment. On the other hand, the child's natural strides toward independence may evoke parental feelings of abandonment.

However, it is critical to remember that parenting is a learning experience for both the child and the parent. The avoidant parent can learn to negotiate their concerns with awareness and assistance, resulting in a profound, nurturing relationship with their child.

This process may necessitate professional assistance, support groups, and ongoing self-awareness. However, the rewards — a deep and meaningful bond with one's child — make the trip worthwhile.

The Cycle of Avoidance: Generation to Generation

While individual experiences influence attachment patterns, they frequently contain echoes of previous generations. The interaction of one's parents, as well as the emotional atmosphere of one's childhood, all play important roles in forming attachment patterns.

Children who grow up in families where avoidant attachment is prevalent often associate distance with safety. They learn early on that it is best to bury emotions and that vulnerability leads to pain.

Without action, these tendencies can continue, establishing a generational loop. The child of an avoidantly attached parent may develop similar traits as an adult, prolonging the cycle.

However, raising awareness can help to disrupt the cycle. Recognizing patterns, understanding their causes, and seeking therapeutic solutions might pave the way for transformation. Every generation can rewrite the story to raise their children in a more emotionally caring environment.

Short-lived Romances and Their Underlying Causes

The dating scene might be especially difficult for the avoidantly attached. While the earliest phases of the relationship, typified by mystery and distance, may be easy to handle, complications frequently arise as the relationship deepens.

The demands of intimacy, as well as the vulnerabilities of closeness, frequently result in short-lived romances. When a partner believes the connection is strengthening, the avoidant person may withdraw, leaving confusion and heartache in their wake.

Deep-seated anxieties lurk behind these patterns: engulf-ment, loss of identity, and vulnerability. However, these protec-tive habits frequently cause anguish for the individual and their companions.

Recognizing these tendencies, understanding their causes, and getting help can lead to more o more fulfilling romantic experiences. While the path may be difficult, the results — deep, lasting connections — are well worth the effort.

The Role of Communication Breakdowns

Communication is essential in any relationship. However, it can be a minefield for the overly connected. It can be difficult to express needs, share vulnerabilities, or even navigate disagreements.

Instead of open dialogue, there is often seclusion. Instead of voicing dissatisfaction, there is silence. Over time, these habits can cause substantial communication disruptions, weakening the foundations of a partnership.

However, underneath this avoidance is a strong yearning: to be understood, to be welcomed. Bridging the gap between this desire and the defensive mechanisms that inhibit open commu-nication is the challenge.

These communication barriers can be broken down with intentional effort, counseling, and mutual understanding. Part-ners can learn to express themselves and listen to one another, resulting in a partnership that feeds on openness and under-standing.

Sexuality and Intimacy Challenges

Sexuality, with its inherent vulnerabilities and demands for closeness, can be an especially challenging terrain for the avoidantly attached. While physical closeness may be easily handled, emotional connection may be elusive during such moments.

This duality frequently perplexes spouses. The act, intended to be a union of bodies and souls, may appear one-dimensional, without the emotional depth that characterizes true closeness.

The act of making love may be another arena where the avoidantly attached defend their vulnerabilities, fearful that deep emotional connection may cage them and make them vulnerable to pain.

This chasm, however, can be crossed with patience, under-standing, and open communication. Sexuality can become an arena in which both couples interact, not just physically but emotionally, forming a deep and lasting bond.

Rebuilding Trust: A Difficult Task

Once broken, trust is difficult to repair. This endeavor might be especially difficult for the avoidantly attached, who frequently battle with trust concerns.

Every slight, every perceived rejection is often exaggerated, undermining the fragile trust they may have developed. Their disengagement, avoidance, and emotional unavailability tenden-cies might put extra strain on this trust.

However, inside this struggle lies the opportunity for development. Because it is only through rebuilding trust that both partners can genuinely understand each other, identifying their anxieties, vulnerabilities, and strengths.

The trip may be long and filled with setbacks and hardships. Trust may be rebuilt, stronger, and more resilient, with patience, empathy, and a commitment to growth.

Can Avoidants and Securely Attached Individuals Coexist?

A balance is at the heart of stable attachment: independence and intimacy, self-reliance, and interdependence. Can this equilibrium survive with avoidant attachment patterns?

While difficult, the answer is positive. While the early phases may be difficult, with the securely attached spouse frequently feeling perplexed by their avoidant partner's tendencies, there is room for growth.

With their inherent sense of self-worth and ability to manage intimacy, the secure individual can provide the avoidant partner with a safe zone: a space to explore their weaknesses without fear.

In turn, the avoidant individual can inject elements of autonomy and self-reliance into the relationship due to their fierce sense of independence.

This combination, like any other, necessitates work, understanding, and open communication. However, with these in place, avoidants and securely attached persons can cohabit and thrive, resulting in a meaningful and liberating connection.

FIVE
HEALING FROM AVOIDANT ATTACHMENT

The Path to Self-Awareness

Recognition is frequently the first step toward healing. For many people who have avoidant attachment patterns, the first step is to recognize that their approach to relationships and intimacy is a coping mechanism developed over time. This revelation is not always simple. It calls into question firmly-held assumptions about oneself, exposing hidden vulnerabilities.

The journey to self-awareness is both intellectual and emotional in nature. It entails reading, researching, and understanding the complexities of attachment theory. But it's also about introspection: looking back at one's life, finding patterns, and tracing them back to their roots.

This trip can be aided by personal diaries, introspective notebooks, or even chats with close confidantes. The goal is not self-criticism but rather understanding. Only through understanding can true transformation begin.

This journey is frequently painful as buried emotions arise. However, with each layer of understanding comes a sense of liberty, a step closer to true, rewarding connections.

The Role of Therapy and Counseling

Professional intervention, such as therapy or counseling, is frequently invaluable on the road to recovery from avoidant attachment. Trained therapists provide a neutral, nonjudgmental environment where one's habits can be deconstructed, understood, and treated.

Sessions may include discussions on prior relationships, early childhood experiences, or even current problems. The therapist frequently serves as a mirror, revealing patterns that could otherwise go unnoticed.

Therapy entails more than just talking. It provides skills, methods, and coping processes to help break bad habits. The emphasis is on holistic recovery, whether through cognitive-behavioral approaches, mindfulness exercises, or story therapy.

For many people, treatment is not a one-time fix. It's a never-ending adventure, a safe haven for them as they face the obstacles of changing deeply ingrained patterns.

What Is Attachment-Based Therapy?

Attachment-based therapy focuses deeply on an individual's attachment style, tracing it back to early childhood experiences and understanding how it influences current actions. It is based on the assumption that our early attachment experiences define our relationship blueprints, influencing how we approach intimacy, trust, and connection.

During these sessions, therapists frequently investigate early parent-child relationships, seeking patterns that may have given rise to avoidant behaviors. This isn't about assigning guilt but about understanding.

Attachment-based treatment relies heavily on narratives. The emotions associated with these narratives, as well as the beliefs that stem from them, all provide insights into one's attachment style.

With understanding, the goal then shifts to rewriting these narratives. This entails questioning deeply held beliefs, presenting alternate interpretations, and gradually constructing a more solid relational pattern.

Rewriting the Attachment Script

Change is difficult, especially when it includes deeply ingrained behaviors. However, it is not impossible. Rewriting one's attachment script is intentionally choosing a different narrative that is more in line with one's genuine self.

It all starts with acknowledgment. When an avoidant tendency emerges, whether the desire to withdraw or avoid closeness, it's important to pause and recognize the impulse.

Then comes introspection. What is causing this reaction? Is it a current circumstance or a recollection from the past casting its shadow? Fears that drive avoidant actions are frequently rooted in past experiences rather than present ones.

Following comprehension, the emphasis moves to response. It's about choosing a different reaction that matches one's aims of developing deeper, more honest connections rather than submitting to age-old patterns.

With constant effort, these new answers become the norm, resulting in a profound shift in one's relationships and self-image.

Mindfulness and Meditation in Healing

The ancient disciplines of mindfulness and meditation are potent tools in the healing journey from avoidant attachment. These techniques are fundamentally about presence, about totally immersing oneself in the present moment, free of past baggage or future fears.

This presence can be transforming for the avoidantly attached. Instead of being governed by previous traumas or future worries, they learn to navigate the present, forming deep and honest connections.

Mindfulness activities promote emotional awareness, such as focused breathing, guided visualization, and even body scans. Rather than repressing or fleeing them, one learns to sit with them, understand, and finally master them.

Consistent meditation, on the other hand, provides a safe haven in which to confront and recover from past traumas. These activities, over time, not only aid in the healing of avoidant tendencies but also in the development of a more centered, true self.

The Power of Vulnerability

For a long time, vulnerability was associated with weakness. However, it is possibly the most powerful tool in relationships. It's the bridge that connects souls, allowing for deep, authentic connections.

Accepting vulnerability can be difficult for the avoidantly attached. Years of associating proximity with pain have resulted in the construction of walls to protect individuals from possible harm and genuine connection.

The process of accepting vulnerability is slow. It's about taking tiny actions, such as sharing a personal experience, expressing a worry, or reaching out in times of uncertainty.

Every act of vulnerability calls into question the avoidant narrative, demonstrating that intimacy does not always result in misery. That, in fact, can lead to profound joy, understanding, and connection.

Over time, with consistent efforts, vulnerability ceases to be a threat, transforming into a strength, a tool that paves the path to fulfilling relationships.

Building a Support System

There is no such thing as a solitary healing journey. It necessitates assistance, a tribe that understands, empathizes, and assists in the transition process. Building this support network is critical for those recovering from avoidant attachment.

This system could include close friends who understand the difficulties of avoidant connection. It could include support groups where people discuss their experiences, bringing insights and friendship.

Then there's the role of mentors, therapists, counselors, or even those who have successfully negotiated the difficulties of avoidant attachment. Their views, strategies, and mere presence provide both comfort and direction.

A strong support structure serves as a safety net, a place to go in times of doubt or relapse. It serves as a reminder that the path, while personal, is not solitary.

The Importance of Self-compassion

Self-compassion is at the heart of healing from any deep-seated pattern. It's the salve that heals old wounds and the anchor that keeps one grounded in times of uncertainty. Self-compassion is critical for persons suffering from avoidant attachment.

It's about admitting that the avoidant behaviors were developed for protection rather than malice. It's about realizing that every withdrawal, every act of avoidance, was done to protect one's fragile self.

With this understanding comes forgiveness. Instead of chastising oneself for past habits, embrace them and recognize them as survival strategies.

There will be periods of relapse, of reverting to old patterns, as one embarks on the path to change. Self-compassion is essential in this situation, reminding one that the path is about progress, not perfection.

Overcoming the Fear of Rejection

Real or perceived rejection is frequently at the root of avoidant actions. The deep-seated fear of not being good enough, of being discarded or dismissed, frequently drives patterns of withdrawal and evasion.

Addressing this fear is critical in the healing process. It entails challenging these ideas, obtaining information that contradicts them, and developing a strong sense of self-worth that is not dependent on external validation.

Every connection, every relationship provides an opportunity. Rather than viewing them through the prism of potential rejection, they might be viewed as opportunities for connection, understanding, and progress.

With conscious effort, the fear of rejection fades over time, replaced by confidence in one's intrinsic worth and the value they contribute to relationships.

Embracing Love and Intimacy

The ability to accept love and intimacy is the culmination of the healing path. It is about making deep, real, and meaningful connections.

This does not imply a lack of fear or doubt. But it's about navigating these feelings and seeing them for what they are: relics of a previous story.

Embracing love entails taking chances. It's about opening up and letting others see one's true self, with all its flaws and talents.

It's about reciprocal development, about creating a relationship in which both parties grow, supported by the love and understanding they share.

This hug is both an end and a beginning for those recovering from avoidant attachment. It is the climax of a journey of self-awareness and healing, as well as the start of a life filled with profound connections and genuine love.

SIX
CASE STUDIES: REAL STORIES OF AVOIDANT ATTACHMENT

Jane: Independence or Fear?

Jane grew up hearing stories about how she never cried as a baby and was always fiercely independent. This became her identity over time. She took satisfaction in not needing anyone and facing life's obstacles alone. Relationships? They were good but not required. So she reasoned.

It wasn't until she was in her mid-30s that she began to doubt this tale. Was her "independence" genuine or a bulwark against impending heartbreak? She began to suspect the latter, especially after her third breakup due to "emotional unavailability."

Jane discovered, in retrospect, that her "strength" was frequently an escape route. Any signs of vulnerability in her lovers prompted her to withdraw, labeling them "too needy."

It wasn't about them at all, it was all about her. A childhood marked by an emotionally distant mother and a series of broken promises instilled a deep fear of relying on anyone.

Jane's initial step was to recognize this pattern. The road ahead would be filled with counseling, contemplation, and the long, agonizing process of allowing vulnerability into her life. The façade of fake independence broke with each step, paving the way for genuine connections.

Alex: The Serial Dater

Alex had it all: dates, flings, and brief romances. He'd been in more romances than most individuals in their lifetimes by the time he was 27. But if you asked him about a long-term, committed relationship, he'd draw a blank.

Alex's charm made him irresistible. But beneath that charisma was a fundamental fear of genuine closeness. Every relationship had an expiration date, frequently decided by Alex's internal alert that said "too close."

The patterns were eerily similar. Intense attraction, passionate beginnings, and a swift exit as emotional connection increased. The explanations ranged from "not the right fit," "need some space," to the usual "it's not you, it's me."

Friends referred to him as commitment-phobic. But deep down, Alex was battling scars from a tumultuous childhood marked by abandonment. In his mind, commitment was synonymous with impending abandonment.

Alex recognized his habits only after a particularly difficult breakup and ensuing period of contemplation. The road to recovery was bumpy, punctuated by relapses and heartbreak.

But with time and therapy, Alex learned to stay, build, and truly connect.

Kim and Lee: The Avoidant-Anxious Rollercoaster

Kim and Lee's relationship was a rollercoaster ride. Exciting highs are followed by heartbreaking lows. To outsiders, their love was intense. But beneath the surface, it was a textbook case of the avoidant-anxious dynamic.

Kim, with her avoidant tendencies, cherished her space. Every time Lee sought closeness, she'd withdraw, seeking refuge in her independence. Lee, on the other hand, craved intimacy. Her anxious attachment made her clingy, perpetually seeking validation and reassurance.

Their patterns influenced one another. Kim's disengagement would heighten Lee's anxiety, causing her to clutch even more tightly. This would push Kim even further away, perpetuating the cycle.

Arguments were common, and they frequently revolved around issues of space, trust, and commitment. Breakups were common, but so were passionate reconciliations.

It was during couples' therapy that they began to recognize their toxic patterns. Understanding each other's attachment styles was the first step. The path ahead involved setting boundaries, cultivating trust, and learning to navigate their individual fears in a way that nurtured rather than strained their bond.

Carlos: Healing Through Therapy

Carlos, a successful lawyer, appeared to have it all. But, beneath his confident façade, he harbored deep-seated concerns of intimacy and vulnerability, which sprang from a strained relationship with his father.

Carlos was continually seeking validation from his emotionally unavailable father as a child. However, approval was scarce, and Carlos frequently felt inadequate, despite his accomplishments. This emptiness manifested in his adult relationships, where he continually feared rejection and inadequacy.

Carlos sought treatment only after his marriage fell apart, owing mostly to his emotional remoteness. He revisited childhood memories throughout the sessions and recognized the origins of his avoidant habits.

Attachment-based therapy was crucial. Carlos recalled his childhood experiences to understand and heal from them. He gradually learned to open up, be vulnerable, and connect with his wife.

His journey was not without challenges, including moments of self-doubt. However, with constant counseling and the assistance of his spouse, Carlos was able to transition from avoidance to stable attachment, rebuilding his marriage and self-worth.

Natasha: Rebuilding a Shattered Trust

Natasha's early twenties were defined by a turbulent relationship that shattered her trust. When it was over, she determined never to let anyone near her again. And she kept her promise for years.

Every possible relationship was scrutinized with skepticism. Any evidence of contradiction was regarded as a red flag, resulting in quick exits. Natasha's defenses were fortified with the bricks of past treachery.

Loneliness crept in as the years passed by. But her longing for connection was surpassed by her fear of being harmed again until she met Jake, who began to chip away at her walls with patience and understanding.

The journey was not easy. Natasha's old traumas frequently resurfaced, causing her to withdraw. However, Jake's persistent support, paired with counseling, assisted her in confronting and healing from her past.

It took time to reestablish trust once it had been damaged. But, with time, understanding, and constant work, Natasha was able to overcome her concerns and embrace love and vulnerability once more.

David: From Avoidance to Secure Attachment

David's motto was straightforward: "Rely on no one but yourself." He'd done it for most of his life, managing problems with stoic independence. Relationships were a part of his life, but they were on his terms, with emotional detachment and fear of actual connection.

His avoidance resulted from a childhood filled with unpredictable caregivers. They were present one minute, showering him with affection, and then they were gone, leaving him to fend for himself. This insecurity created a feeling that people could not be trusted.

But as David approached his late thirties, a gnawing loneliness set in. He began to wonder about his routines, about his persistent need for distance. Therapy was a watershed moment for him.

He delved into his past through sessions, gaining insight into the causes of his avoidant habits. He became aware of his habits after learning about attachment theories.

David began the slow process of change with his newfound understanding. It entailed testing his views, accepting vulnerability, and forging deep, genuine connections. The journey was difficult, with frequent relapses, but with time, David moved from avoidance to secure attachment, developing rewarding relationships based on trust and genuine intimacy.

Sarah: Parenting with Avoidant Tendencies

Sarah had always taken pride in raising independent children. "They don't need to be coddled," she would often say. But underneath this assumption was her own fear of intimacy, expressing itself in her parenting style.

Her children, while independent, frequently expressed feelings of emotional detachment. They felt abandoned, yearning for the connection that their mother was unable to provide.

Sarah's childhood was characterized by neglect. Emotional support was lacking, so she built barriers and learned to fend for herself. She was unknowingly repeating the same routines with her children.

A run-in with her eldest, who accused her of being "emotionally absent," served as a wake-up call for Sarah. She sought therapy, delving into her past and recognizing her avoidant patterns.

Sarah began to transform as a result of her newfound awareness. She learned to show her love and provide her children with the emotional support they needed. The road wasn't easy, and it was fraught with self-doubt, but Sarah rebuilt her relationship with her children, ensuring that the cycle of avoidance didn't continue.

Mark: The Corporate Climber's Emotional Void

Mark had an amazing resume. He'd worked his way up the corporate ladder as a senior executive at a well-known firm. Behind his professional achievement, though, was an emotional hole, a deep-seated fear of connection that manifested in his personal life.

Mark's escape was work. Long hours gave him a legitimate reason to avoid social gatherings, family gatherings, and intimate moments. His relationships were fleeting, typically with workaholics, ensuring that emotional depth was avoided.

But as accolades poured in, Mark's internal world crumbled. Loneliness was palpable, and it led to spells of sadness. A close friend's involvement pushed him into counseling, which initially opposed but later accepted.

Through sessions, he recognized his avoidant tendencies, understanding their origins in a childhood marked by emotional neglect. Work was his defense mechanism, a way to avoid confronting his fears.

Mark began to discover a sense of equilibrium through treatment. He learned to prioritize connections, accept vulnerability, and fill the emotional gap that had loomed over his life. His recovery journey impacted not only his personal life but also his professional approach, transforming him into a more empathic and balanced leader.

Lena: Cultural Pressures and Avoidance

Stoicism was highly valued in Lena's culture. Emotions, particularly unpleasant ones, were to be controlled rather than expressed. Growing up, Lena learned to hide her emotions, putting on a brave face even in moments of vulnerability.

These behaviors got ingrained as she moved into maturity. Emotional distance defined relationships. Lena feared that any sign of vulnerability would be interpreted as weakness, leading to rejection.

Her lovers frequently complained about her "coldness" or unwillingness to connect. However, Lena was caught in a cultural trap, torn between her intrinsic craving for connection and societal pressures to stay "strong."

Lena's turning point was a cross-cultural connection. Her spouse, who comes from a culture that values emotional expressiveness, was perplexed by her distance. Their differences caused friction, but they also exposed Lena to new ways of relating.

Lena began to question her deeply-held ideas after receiving therapy and support. She learned to communicate her feelings, embrace vulnerability, and form genuine friendships that transcended cultural norms. It was a voyage of unlearning and constructing a new story that valued emotional depth and genuine intimacy.

Sam: The Journey of Self-acceptance

Sam's life was defined by relentless deception. He avoided social gatherings, intimate moments, and deep conversations. Friends termed him the "mystery man" since he was always around yet emotionally detached.

Sam's avoidance was motivated by deep-seated self-esteem concerns. He was convinced that if people fully knew him, they would reject him. So, he wore masks, presenting personas that kept people at arm's length.

Relationships were fleeting. Sam would leave whenever partners sought depth, fearing exposure. For years, this pattern persisted, leaving a trail of broken hearts, including his own.

Sam's journey to self-acceptance began with a chance meeting with a therapist at a wellness retreat. He began counseling, exploring his background, and overcoming his fears.

Sam gradually realized his own worth. He learned to remove his masks and expose his own self, warts and all. And, to his amazement, people embraced him rather than rejected him.

His path was not straight and was frequently interrupted by moments of self-doubt. However, with the help of counseling and a supportive community, Sam could accept himself, enjoy love and intimacy, and fully connect with those around him.

SEVEN

STRATEGIES FOR PARTNERS OF AVOIDANT INDIVIDUALS

Understanding, Not Blaming

When dealing with an avoidant person, it's easy to misinterpret their actions as a lack of interest or concern. However, it is crucial to recognize that these behaviors are frequently motivated by deep-seated concerns and previous traumas rather than malice or apathy.

Grasping the root causes of avoidant attachment can be a game-changer. It allows partners to approach the situation with empathy rather than frustration. Delving into the world of attachment theories, reading books, or even attending workshops can shed light on the intricacies of this attachment style.

Miscommunications can worsen avoidant tendencies. As a result, information becomes a powerful instrument, enabling partners to handle obstacles effectively.

Partners can help avoidant individuals open up, communicate their worries, and take baby steps toward vulnerability by creating an understanding environment. It is not about excusing behaviors but about understanding where they came from.

Tolerating toxic behaviors does not imply shifting from blame to understanding. It's about confronting problems compassionately and creating a relationship environment that promotes growth and healing.

Navigating the Push-Pull Dynamics

The push-pull dynamic is common in interactions with avoidant people. They may appear invested one moment and then withdraw, causing confusion and unease.

The first step is to recognize this pattern. It is critical to recognize that this is not a reflection of your worth or desirability but rather a representation of the avoidant's internal struggle with intimacy.

When confronted with this dynamic, it is important not to react with desperation or clinginess since this might intensify the problem. Giving space while articulating your feelings, on the other hand, can achieve the proper balance.

Avoidants often fear engulfment, feeling trapped in intimacy. By recognizing this, partners can navigate the push-pull sensitively, ensuring that space doesn't translate into emotional distance.

It's a delicate balance that necessitates patience and understanding. Over time, with consistent efforts and communication, this dynamic can be managed, fostering a more stable relationship environment.

Encouraging Open Communication

Open communication is essential in any relationship, but it is especially important when one partner has avoidant tendencies.

Creating a safe space for dialogue is essential. It's about creating an atmosphere where both parties feel heard, validated, and understood. Because of their worries, avoidants may struggle with open communication. As a result, it is critical to encourage, rather than compel, dialogue.

Active listening is quite important. It is not only about hearing words, but also about recognizing unspoken emotions, worries, and weaknesses.

Check-ins can be useful. Regular dialogues about the state of the relationship, its obstacles, and ideas to improve can help to keep problems from festering.

However, it is crucial to approach such discussions with tact. Avoidants may see them as conflicts, leading to even more withdrawal. It can help to frame them as collaborative dialogues, emphasizing the desire to understand and grow together.

Seeking Professional Help as a Couple

Therapy isn't a sign of a broken relationship but a commitment to growth, healing, and understanding. Couples therapy can be transformative when working with an avoidant person.

A professional can offer insights, tools, and strategies tailored to the relationship's unique challenges. They can shed light on the underlying causes of avoidant behavior, allowing for more understanding and empathy.

Couples therapy provides a neutral ground, a safe environment for couples to express their concerns, fears, and aspirations. It can be a platform for avoidant people to address their problems, delve into their past, and begin the healing process.

Individual sessions can supplement joint sessions. While the avoidant spouse investigates the complexities of their attachment style, the other partner can explore their feelings, challenges, and coping mechanisms.

It is critical to select the correct therapist. It's essential finding someone with whom both partners can connect, someone who knows the complexities of attachment theories and can lead the couple on their path to a healthy relationship.

Recognizing Triggers and Patterns

Understanding the triggers of an avoidant partner might help to prevent misunderstandings and disputes. Everyone has specific events, words, or acts that elicit strong emotional responses. These frequently revolve around intimacy and vulnerability for avoidant people.

Recognizing these triggers allows partners to approach situations with caution, avoiding unwittingly pushing the avoidant further into withdrawal.

Once detected, patterns of behavior can be addressed. Understanding why an avoidant partner pulls away after moments of intimacy can help the other partner negotiate such circumstances better.

In times of quiet, discussing these patterns might be beneficial. It's about working together to disrupt negative cycles and promote growth and understanding.

However, it's crucial to approach such discussions without blame. It's not about pointing fingers but understanding each other better, ensuring that the relationship thrives.

Building Trust Incrementally

Trust is the foundation of any relationship, yet it can be difficult to establish with avoidant people. Their history may be marred by betrayals, contradictions, or emotional abuse, making trust a difficult task.

However, just because trust has been shattered does not mean it can't be repaired. It's a gradual process that requires consistent actions, understanding, and patience.

Small gestures have a big impact. Being there in vulnerable moments, offering support, understanding, and compassion, can lay the groundwork for trust.

It is impossible to overestimate the value of open communication. Both partners can develop a relationship built on honesty and mutual respect by communicating their worries, aspirations, and feelings.

It is critical to acknowledge setbacks and occasions when trust may wane. However, trust can be developed with perseverance, understanding, and a commitment to progress, leading to a satisfying partnership.

The Role of Patience and Persistence

It's not always easy to navigate a relationship with an avoidant person. Patience, understanding, and steadfast persistence are required.

It is important to remember that change does not occur overnight. Healing, comprehension, and growth are all gradual processes frequently interrupted by setbacks. Positive changes can, however, emerge with persistence.

Small triumphs might help to boost motivation. Recognizing when the avoidant partner opens up, shares, or addresses their anxieties can be quite powerful in promoting future growth.

Avoidant people may withdraw, especially when they are vulnerable. But patience, as well as giving them room to process their emotions while providing steadfast support, can make a difference.

Finally, it's about appreciating the journey's value and realizing that problems, when met with love, understanding, and patience, can lead to a rewarding, deep, and meaningful relationship.

Finding Balance: Independence and Togetherness

In any relationship, balance is essential. When one spouse has avoidant tendencies, however, finding the correct balance of independence and closeness becomes pivotal.

Avoidant people treasure their independence. This, however, is not a reflection of their devotion or love but rather a representation of their engulfment concerns. Recognizing this can help to avoid misunderstandings.

Finding activities that both partners like, as well as creating moments of togetherness, can help to develop positive associations with intimacy. It's about making memories, developing a shared story, and strengthening the fabric of the connection.

Respecting the demand for independence is also crucial.

Allowing the avoidant partner space without misinterpreting it as rejection might help to build trust and understanding.

It is not always simple to strike this equilibrium. Open communication, mutual understanding, and mutual respect are essential. Independence and togetherness can coexist peacefully with effort and understanding.

Establishing Healthy Boundaries

In any relationship, boundaries are vital. They make certain that both partners are appreciated, valued, and understood. Setting limits becomes even more important when dealing with an avoidant person.

It's about learning one other's requirements, limitations, and comfort zones. Boundaries for avoidant people may revolve around the need for distance, the fear of being engulfed, or the desire to retain a sense of independence.

Setting limits is not a one-time event. It's a continuous process that evolves as the connection grows and changes.

The importance of open communication cannot be overstated. By discussing limits, both couples can ensure they're on the same page, avoiding misunderstandings and disputes.

However, it is critical to approach boundaries with flexibility. Relationships, while providing a framework, are dynamic. Being willing to revisit, discuss, and adjust boundaries can promote growth and mutual respect.

Self-care for the Non-Avoidant Partner

Being in a relationship with someone who avoids people can be emotionally draining. As a result, self-care becomes critical for the non-avoidant partner.

Self-care is more than just spa days and getaways. It is about understanding and meeting your emotional needs. This could include seeking treatment, joining support groups, or simply participating in activities that promote serenity and contentment.

Maintaining an identity outside of the relationship is critical. Pursuing hobbies, retaining friendships, and focusing on personal improvement can provide respite, preventing relationship issues from becoming overwhelming.

Seeking help is critical. Friends, relatives, or therapists can provide insights, a listening ear, and solutions for navigating the unique issues of the relationship.

Finally, self-care is about recognizing your worth, guaranteeing emotional fulfillment, and being prepared to manage the challenges and rewards that come with being involved with an avoidant person.

EIGHT
SOCIETAL IMPACTS AND AVOIDANT ATTACHMENT

The Influence of Modern Dating Culture

Technology, societal norms, and shifting expectations have all had a significant impact on modern dating. Dating apps have popularized the concept of abundance and choice, often at the expense of depth and commitment.

This never-ending whirlwind of potential matches can exacerbate avoidant tendencies. Those afraid of intimacy benefit from the ease of swiping left or ghosting someone without confrontation.

Many modern dating relationships are also transient, which corresponds to avoidant patterns. Commitment is frequently delayed, and relationships can remain ambiguous, allowing avoidant people to maintain emotional distance.

However, it is critical to understand that while modern dating culture may facilitate avoidant behaviors, it does not necessarily cause them. Avoidant attachment styles result from early life experiences played out in the dating world.

One could argue that the lack of need to commit and the abundance of options has allowed avoidant people to blend in, making their behavior the norm rather than the exception.

The 'hookup culture' frequently lacks emotional depth, making it a haven for avoidants. They can engage in surface-level relationships without confronting their fears by avoiding deep emotional connections.

However, it is a double-edged sword. The platforms that enable such behavior also highlight the loneliness and lack of genuine connection that many people experience, emphasizing the importance of genuine intimacy.

Avoidant Attachment in the Workplace

Self-sufficiency, independence, and the ability to work without excessive emotional involvement are frequently rewarded in the business world. On the surface, it appears that avoidant people would thrive in such a setting.

Their natural tendency toward self-reliance and reluctance to rely on others is frequently perceived as a strength, identifying them as go-getters or lone wolves who get the job done.

However, relationships do exist in the workplace. Teamwork, collaboration, and effective communication are critical; avoidant behaviors can stymie these processes.

Avoidant people may struggle with feedback because they interpret it as criticism or rejection. This can stifle development and foster misunderstandings.

Furthermore, while they may excel in roles requiring little to no interpersonal interaction, leadership roles requiring emotional intelligence, mentorship, and guidance can be difficult.

It's a complicated scenario. On the one hand, their desire for independence can spur creativity and self-starting initiatives. On the other hand, the very essence of modern workplaces, collaboration, and open communication, can be difficult.

Companies and organizations must recognize these dynamics and provide support, training, and an environment where emotional intelligence is valued as highly as any other skill.

The Role of Social Media and Digital Communication

Communication has taken on new dimensions in the age of the Internet. While it has helped to bridge gaps and bring the world closer together, it has also added layers of complexity to human interactions.

Digital communication can be both a blessing and a curse for avoidant people. Social media platforms provide a semblance of connection without the depth of face-to-face inter-actions, which aligns with their proclivity to maintain emotional distance.

The curated lives displayed on social media can also exacer-bate feelings of inadequacy or fear of judgment, driving avoidant people even deeper into their shells.

With its emojis, gifs, and lack of tone, digital communica-tion frequently lacks the nuance of face-to-face conversations. Misunderstandings can occur, and for someone with avoidant tendencies, they can serve as additional reasons to withdraw.

There is, however, a silver lining. Online communities, forums, and support groups can allow avoidant people to share, learn about their attachment style, and even start their healing journey.

The key lies in mindful engagement. Recognizing the pitfalls and potential of digital communication can assist avoidant individuals in effectively navigating the online world.

The "Lone Hero" Trope in Media and its Impacts

For a long time, cinema, literature, and television have romanticized the "lone hero" - an individual who, despite all odds, overcomes challenges without the help of others. While the story is compelling, there are consequences.

This trope validates avoidant behavior by portraying it as heroic rather than normal. The lone wolf, who doesn't 'need' anyone, becomes an ideal, driving avoidant people deeper into their belief systems.

Such narratives have the potential to shape societal expectations. Independence is praised, while vulnerability, frequently a path to genuine connection and intimacy, is viewed as a flaw.

Furthermore, these stories frequently end with the lone hero finding love or connection, reinforcing the idea that, despite their avoidance, they still deserve love without making any emotional adjustments.

In an ideal world, the media would recognize its power and portrays a more balanced view of relationships, emphasizing the power of vulnerability, collaboration, and mutual support.

Avoidant Attachment and Community Participation

Community participation, whether in local groups, clubs, or neighborhood initiatives, is frequently about collaboration, mutual support, and connection - all of which can be difficult for avoidant people.

Their reluctance to form deep connections can stymie active participation. While they may participate, they frequently remain on the outskirts, hesitant to take on roles that require deeper interpersonal interactions.

Avoidant people may struggle with community feedback as well, misinterpreting it as personal criticism. This may discourage them from participating actively or taking on leadership roles.

Communities, on the other hand, can play an important role in their healing process. A welcoming, understanding community can provide a platform for them to engage, form connections at their own pace, and confront and navigate their fears.

Recognizing the signs of avoidant attachment and fostering an inclusive, supportive environment can make a significant difference for community leaders.

The Education System and Avoidant Students

For avoidant students, the education system can be challenging with its structured environments and emphasis on grades. Their fear of criticism or rejection can manifest as a fear of receiving poor grades or feedback.

Students who avoid group projects or activities that require collaboration may also struggle. Their tendency to maintain emotional distance can be misinterpreted as aloofness or disinterest.

Teachers and educators play an important role in this. Recognizing the symptoms of avoidant attachment and providing support, understanding, and a safe environment can help.

When given the right support, avoidant students can thrive, transforming their natural tendency toward self-reliance into academic strengths.

It's about finding a happy medium between pushing them to confront their fears and providing a safety net of support and understanding.

The Broader Economic and Social Impacts

On a larger scale, avoidant attachment can have economic and social consequences. Avoidant people may avoid jobs that require interpersonal interactions, limiting their professional options.

Their reluctance to form deep connections can also impact community initiatives, resulting in decreased community participation and cohesion.

On the financial front, they may prefer solo ventures or roles that require little collaboration, influencing team dynamics in larger organizations.

Socially, a sizable proportion of the population exhibiting avoidant tendencies can lead to decreased community cohesion, lower community participation, and even negative effects on the broader societal fabric.

However, it is critical to recognize that each individual,

including those who avoid, brings unique strengths to the table. Society can effectively harness these strengths by fostering environments of understanding, support, and inclusion.

Pop Culture's Love-Avoidance Paradox

A paradox is frequently depicted in popular culture. On the one hand, it romanticizes love and depicts it as the ultimate goal. On the other hand, it portrays love as turbulent and difficult, often aligning with the fears of avoidant people.

This paradox can aggravate avoidant behaviors. While they may long for the romanticized version of love, the challenges, which are frequently exaggerated in pop culture narratives, can reinforce their fears.

While songs, movies, and literature about heartbreak, betrayal, or the difficulties of love may resonate with many, they can also deter avoidant people from seeking genuine connections.

It's a complicated scenario in which pop culture not only reflects but also shapes societal beliefs and norms. Recognizing its power and portraying balanced, realistic narratives can have an impact.

The Pros and Cons of an Independent Society

Many characteristics of avoidant people are shared by an independent society that values self-reliance, innovation, and individuality. Their natural desire for independence and self-sufficiency is frequently praised.

However, while independence is beneficial in many ways, it

can also discourage genuine connection, community participation, and mutual support.

On the other hand, a society that values both independence and interdependence can thrive. It strikes a balance by valuing individual strengths while also emphasizing the importance of community, collaboration, and mutual support.

In such a society, avoidant individuals can have their strengths recognized while also being encouraged and supported to confront and navigate their fears.

Building a More Emotionally Connected World

Building emotional connections becomes critical in a world that often appears fragmented. This journey can be difficult for avoidant people, but it is not impossible.

Societal acceptance of attachment styles, understanding, and support can pave the way. Society can promote healing and growth by de-stigmatizing therapy, increasing mental health awareness, and emphasizing the importance of emotional intelligence.

Community initiatives, educational programs, and corporate policies that acknowledge the complexities of human relationships can all make a difference.

Finally, it is important to recognize that each individual, regardless of attachment style, has something unique to offer. Society can move toward a more emotionally connected future by cultivating an environment of understanding, support, and mutual respect.

NINE
MYTHS AND MISUNDERSTANDINGS

"Avoidant People Don't Want Love"

One common misconception is that avoidant people do not want love. The truth, however, is quite different. Avoidant people, like everyone else, have an innate desire for connection and intimacy.

The distinction is found in their coping mechanisms and fears. They often deal with this desire by maintaining emotional distance, not because they don't want love but because they are afraid of the vulnerability that comes with it.

This fear may be rooted in a variety of past experiences, but it does not negate their innate desire for meaningful connections.

It's also worth noting that their ways of expressing love may differ. While they may struggle to show vulnerability, they can express love through actions, support, and other nonverbal cues.

It is critical for both the individual and their partner to

recognize and understand their unique love language. They can find ways to bridge the emotional gap and cultivate a deeper connection by doing so.

Just as we don't generalize how securely attached people express love, it's unfair and inaccurate to place avoidant people in a rigid framework of expectations.

In essence, avoidant people want love; they just have different ways of getting it and expressing it.

"They're Just Cold and Heartless"

Labeling avoidant people as "cold" or "heartless" is an oversimplification that ignores the complexities of their emotions. Avoidant behavior is about self-protection, not the absence of feelings.

Their apparent coldness is frequently a defense mechanism, a means of protecting themselves from potential emotional pain. This behavior stems from previous experiences that led them to associate vulnerability with pain.

It is critical to distinguish between behavior and intention. While their actions may appear detached, their internal emotional landscape can be just as rich and turbulent as anyone else's.

We risk invalidating their experiences and feelings by labeling them emotionless, making it more difficult for them to open up and heal.

Recognizing their emotional depth and assisting them in navigating it without judgment leads to true understanding and healing.

"Avoidant Attachment Can't Be Changed"

It is a myth that attachment styles are fixed and unchangeable. While early childhood experiences shape attachment styles, the brain's plasticity and the human capacity for change mean these patterns can change.

It is critical to approach this with a realistic attitude. Changing deeply ingrained behavioral patterns takes time, effort, self-awareness, and, in many cases, professional assistance.

There are numerous stories of avoidant people who have progressed to a more secure attachment style through therapy, introspection, and supportive relationships.

Believing that avoidant attachment is permanent not only undermines the work of mental health professionals but also undermines avoidant individuals' resilience and potential.

It's a difficult journey, but the right tools, support, and determination make change possible.

"All Avoidants Had Traumatic Childhoods"

It is a common misconception that all avoidantly attached people had traumatic childhoods. While early childhood experiences have a significant influence on attachment styles, not every avoidant individual has experienced trauma.

Avoidant attachment can result from various situations, including inconsistent caregiving, emotional neglect, or a caregiver's unintentional lack of sensitivity to the child's emotions.

It is also important to note that perceptions of neglect or

inconsistency are subjective. What one child considers neglectful, another may not.

Furthermore, attachment styles can change over time. Adults may develop an avoidant attachment style due to experiences unrelated to their childhood.

Generalizing or assuming the backstory of every avoidant person can lead to misplaced sympathy or unintentional invalidation of their experiences.

"They're Simply Commitment-phobic"

Labeling avoidant people as "commitment-phobic" oversimplifies their emotional landscape. Avoidance of commitment stems from a deep-seated fear of vulnerability rather than a whimsical fear of responsibility.

While it is true that avoidant people may be hesitant to commit, understanding the reasons for this hesitancy is critical. They frequently worry that committing will lead to unrealistic expectations or emotional demands they can't handle.

It's also worth noting that while commitment phobia and avoidant attachment overlap, they're not the same thing. Commitment phobia can exist without being avoidantly attached, and vice versa.

Recognizing this distinction and assisting avoidant individuals in navigating their commitment fears results in true understanding and support.

"Avoidants Can't Be Good Parents"

This is a particularly pernicious myth. Avoidant people, like everyone else, can be loving and supportive parents. Their avoidant attachment style does not preclude them from caring, nurturing, or providing.

While they may struggle with some aspects of parenting, particularly those requiring emotional vulnerability, they also bring unique strengths. Their emphasis on self-reliance, resilience, and independence can benefit their children.

It is critical to recognize that parenting is a learning experience. When avoidant people become parents, they frequently confront their fears and behaviors to provide the best for their children.

Furthermore, they can navigate parenting challenges effectively with awareness, support, and guidance, ensuring a nurturing environment for their children.

"They Don't Need Therapy, Just a Good Partner"

The idea that a good romantic partner can "fix" an avoidant person is not only simplistic but also potentially harmful. While supportive relationships can help avoidant people navigate their fears, putting the onus of healing on a partner is unfair and unrealistic.

Avoidant attachment is rooted in deep behavioral patterns, and addressing them frequently necessitates professional assistance, introspection, and personal work.

The tools, strategies, and understanding required to navigate and confront these patterns are provided by therapy. A supportive partner can help you along the way, but they cannot replace professional guidance.

Moreover, placing the expectation of healing on a relationship can lead to codependency, further complicating the dynamics.

"Avoidant Attachment Is Just an Excuse for Bad Behavior"

Attachment avoidance is an explanation, not an excuse. Understanding why someone behaves the way they do does not absolve them of responsibility or accountability.

Avoidant people must recognize the impact of their actions on others and take steps toward self-awareness and change.

Similarly, partners and close relatives of avoidant people should approach the situation with compassion but not at the expense of their emotional well-being.

Using avoidant attachment as a blanket justification for harmful behavior is counterproductive and can stymie genuine growth and understanding.

"All Introverts are Avoidantly Attached"

It is essential to distinguish between introversion and avoidant attachment. While both may involve a preference for solitude or apprehension in social situations, the underlying reasons and emotions differ.

Introversion is concerned with energy dynamics. Introverts often feel drained in social situations and need time alone to recharge. In contrast, avoidant attachment is motivated by a fear of vulnerability and intimacy.

An extrovert can be avoidantly attached, and an introvert can have a secure attachment style.

Assuming that all introverts are avoidantly attached not only perpetuates stereotypes but also undermines the rich and diverse experiences of both introverts and avoidants.

"Avoidants are Always Loners"

While avoidant people may prefer solitude or avoid intimate relationships, labeling them "loners" is an oversimplification. Their social behavior is motivated by a fear of vulnerability rather than a dislike for company.

Many avoidant people have active social lives, participating in group activities or maintaining superficial friendships. The challenge for them is forming deep, intimate connections.

It is also worth noting that their avoidance is not continuous. They may open up and seek connections with the right triggers, support, or in specific situations.

Understanding the nuances of their social behavior, rather than categorizing them, is essential for genuine understanding and support.

TEN
MOVING FORWARD: A HOPEFUL FUTURE

Recognizing the Spectrum of Attachment

Attachment, like many other aspects of human behavior and emotion, exists on a scale. It is neither binary nor absolute. Everyone has a distinct attachment pattern that is shaped by a combination of genetics, experiences, upbringing, and personal choices.

It is critical to understand this spectrum. It contributes to the development of empathy, patience, and compassion for oneself and others. This recognition provides clarity that there is no "one-size-fits-all" approach to relationships and emotional connections.

Furthermore, it is essential to recognize that one's attachment style is not fixed. Our attachment patterns can change as we grow older. This dynamism offers the possibility of growth, change, and healing.

By recognizing the spectrum, we promote a more inclusive

and understanding society where people feel seen, recognized, and validated for their experiences.

Accepting the variety of human connections, relationships, and emotions allows for richer, deeper, and more authentic bonds.

The Role of Society in Nurturing Secure Attachments

Individual experiences are heavily influenced by society. Societal structures influence how people perceive, understand, and engage in relationships, from the family unit to educational institutions, media representations, to cultural norms.

A shift in societal values is required to foster secure attachments. Promoting consistent, empathetic, and tuned-in caregiving from infancy can lay the groundwork for secure attachment patterns.

Furthermore, educational systems can incorporate emotional literacy and awareness into curricula, ensuring that children have the tools they need to navigate their emotional world.

The media can help by highlighting diverse, healthy relationships, challenging stereotypes, and presenting a balanced picture of human connections.

The fundamental understanding at the heart of these efforts is that nurturing secure attachments benefits society as a whole, leading to more empathetic, understanding, and cohesive communities.

The Power of Awareness and Education

Power comes from knowledge. By raising awareness about attachment theories, patterns, and their implications, we give people the tools to understand themselves and their relationships better.

Education debunks myths and provides a clear, empathetic understanding of the challenges and strengths associated with avoidant attachment.

Awareness campaigns, workshops, seminars, and educational modules can reach various segments of society, resulting in a more comprehensive understanding.

These efforts not only assist avoidant individuals on their path to healing but also provide their partners, families, and friends with the knowledge and tools they need to support them.

Individuals with access to information can make more informed decisions, seek timely interventions, and cultivate healthier, more fulfilling relationships.

Encouraging Emotional Literacy in Children

Emotions are the foundation of human existence. However, emotional literacy is frequently overlooked during the formative years. Encouraging children to recognize, comprehend, and express their emotions is essential for developing healthy attachment patterns.

Children who are emotionally literate grow up to be adults who can navigate the complexities of their inner world and form genuine, deep connections with others.

Through activities, workshops, and curricula, emotional education in schools can lay the groundwork for a more emotionally aware generation.

Parents, caregivers, and educators can be taught to recognize and respond to their children's emotional needs, making them feel seen, heard, and validated.

By emphasizing emotional literacy, we ensure the next generation is better prepared to face relationship challenges, fostering a more emotionally healthy society.

Celebrating Growth and Change

Humans are born with the ability to grow. Celebrating every step, milestone, and breakthrough, no matter how small strengthens faith in the possibility of change.

Recognizing one's journey, efforts, and progress is critical for avoidant people. It motivates, instills hope, and reinforces their belief in their ability to change.

Society can help by creating platforms that share success stories, highlight healing journeys, and provide role models who have successfully navigated the complexities of avoidant attachment.

By celebrating growth, we shift the focus from challenges to opportunities, fostering a more optimistic, hopeful outlook for the future.

Building Bridges: From Avoidance to Acceptance

The path from avoidance to acceptance is not straight. It's full of ups and downs, setbacks and triumphs. Bridge construction between these two states is an ongoing process that requires patience, persistence, and perseverance.

This journey can be aided by support groups, therapy sessions, workshops, and community outreach programs, which provide avoidant individuals with tools, techniques, and a support system.

These bridges aren't just for the avoidant. Understanding and supporting the journey from avoidance to acceptance can benefit partners, family, friends, and society.

By constructing these bridges, we create a network of support, understanding, and compassion, ensuring that no one faces their difficulties alone.

The Future of Attachment Research

Attachment theory has come a long way since its inception. However, the field is constantly evolving, with new research shedding light on the complexities of human connections.

The future holds promise for deeper insights into the nuances of different attachment styles, their implications, and potential interventions.

Emerging research could look into the genetics of attachment, the role of neurobiology, the impact of modern societal structures, and the interaction of culture, upbringing, and personal experiences.

By constantly progressing in this field, we ensure a better understanding and more effective interventions which benefits both individuals and society as a whole.

Embracing All Attachments: An Inclusive Approach

While the emphasis is frequently placed on encouraging secure attachments, it is critical to recognize and validate all attachment patterns. Each style has its advantages and disadvantages, and an inclusive approach ensures that everyone feels seen and understood.

This inclusiveness fosters a sense of belonging, reduces stigma, and promotes empathy and understanding across attachment patterns.

We recognize the diversity of human experiences by embracing all attachments, fostering a society that values, respects, and supports each individual's unique journey.

The Journey of Continuous Self-Improvement

The pursuit of self-awareness and growth is an ongoing one. Every person, regardless of attachment pattern, is constantly striving for self-improvement.

Recognizing this journey, respecting its pace, and providing the tools and support for ongoing growth are all critical.

This emphasis on self-improvement, both individually and collectively, ensures that we are always progressing, evolving, growing, and striving for better, healthier relationships.

Love, Trust, and Connection: A Universal Desire

A universal desire for love, trust, and connection lies at the heart of all human endeavors. This intrinsic need binds humanity regardless of attachment patterns, experiences, or challenges.

Recognizing this universal desire fosters empathy, under-standing, and connection, bridging gaps and fostering genuine bonds.

By focusing on this shared human experience, we can create a world in which everyone, regardless of their individual jour-neys, feels valued, understood, and connected.

Accepting love, trust, and connection as universal desires guarantees a brighter, more cohesive future for all.

CONCLUSION

Reflections on Avoidant Attachment

As we stand at the threshold, looking back at the intricate labyrinth of avoidant attachment, it is critical that we understand its intricate fabric. As we've seen throughout our journey, avoidant attachment is more than just a clinical term or a psychological state; it encompasses how people perceive, react to, and engage with their surroundings.

This attachment style develops due to early experiences and serves as a coping mechanism for navigating life's emotional complexities. However, it does not encompass a person's entire personality. Instead, it is a component of their emotional identity that influences how they connect and relate to others. It's the psyche's attempt to protect itself from perceived emotional harm. As we've seen, the essence of avoidant attachment is self-preservation.

Our investigation has also highlighted the importance of

empathy. We dug deep into this attachment style to understand and connect, not to label or judge. We can see through this understanding lens that every avoidantly attached person has a story, a backdrop against which their behaviors and choices make perfect sense.

Furthermore, by dismantling the various aspects of avoidant attachment, we've shed light on the larger landscape of human connection. Relationships are an interplay of experiences, emotions, and interactions. We invariably shed light on the universal complexities of human connection and our perpetual yearning for belongingness by gaining insight into one specific attachment style.

The Ever-evolving Nature of Human Relationships

Change is the only constant in the vast tapestry of human relationships. Relationship dynamics are constantly changing, from passing acquaintances to deep-rooted familial ties. They change, metamorphose, and sometimes disappear. Despite this shifting landscape, the potential for growth remains unabated.

In many ways, understanding avoidant attachment has emphasized the transformative nature of human connections. What starts as an avoidant pattern with inherent challenges and barriers can evolve into a more secure, connected bond. This transformation is not by chance; it is frequently the result of conscious effort, understanding, and, in some cases, therapeutic intervention.

The dynamism inherent in human connections demonstrates our adaptability and resilience. As we've seen, despite its difficulties, avoidant attachment is not a life sentence. Shifts can occur with understanding, patience, and the right tools, leading to deeper, more fulfilling connections.

The Role of Compassion and Understanding

If there is one recurring theme that has emerged from our journey, it is the critical importance of compassion and understanding. These aren't just words or lofty ideals; they're necessary tools in human connection.

Compassion can be a healing balm for those suffering from avoidant attachment patterns. It provides a safe haven, a judgment-free zone where understanding reigns supreme. Healing, growth, and transformation begin in this compassionate space.

Furthermore, understanding serves as a link between disparate worlds. We start a conversation by attempting to understand the worldview of someone with avoidant tendencies. This conversation, founded on mutual respect and empathy, paves the way for deeper connections.

These twin pillars of compassion and understanding have the potential to challenge and dismantle prevalent misconceptions in a broader societal context. They are antidotes to stigma, promoting a more inclusive and compassionate social fabric.

Celebrating Progress, Not Perfection

Perfection, an often sought-after state, can be a double-edged sword. We may overlook the beauty of progress in our collective quest for perfection. This is especially true in the area of personal development and relationships.

We've stressed the importance of recognizing and celebrating milestones throughout our investigation. Each step is significant, whether it is a breakthrough in therapy, a moment of self-reflection, or an instance where an avoidantly attached individual reaches out.

Focusing on progress ensures that the journey of self-growth and relationship-building remains motivated and recognized. It transforms the story from a looming end goal to a series of fulfilling, enriching moments. This viewpoint is not only empowering but also nurturing, fostering a positive and encouraging environment.

Building Stronger, Deeper Connections

Connections, in their various manifestations, are at the heart of the human experience. Our relationships define our lives, from fleeting interactions to lifelong bonds. This truth has been repeatedly emphasized during our investigation of avoidant attachment.

Regardless of the difficulties posed by avoidant tendencies, the underlying desire remains consistent: a desire for genuine, deep connections. The path to stronger, more fulfilling bonds becomes clear by cultivating an environment of understanding, arming ourselves with knowledge, and approaching relationships with empathy.

Our journey through the world of avoidant attachment has highlighted a universal truth: beneath behaviors, patterns, and tendencies lies an innate human desire for love, acceptance, and connection.

The Potential for Transformation

With its inherent resilience and adaptability, the human spirit is always poised for transformation. Regardless of where one begins, the horizon is brimming with possibilities. This sentiment is especially significant in the context of avoidant attachment.

The possibility of change has been a recurring theme as we navigated the intricate pathways of this attachment style. The journey from avoidance to a more secure attachment becomes possible with awareness, intervention, and a supportive environment.

This possibility of transformation serves as a ray of hope. It demonstrates our innate capacity for growth, change, and evolution. It underscores the belief that tomorrow can be different, brighter, and more connected than today.

Embracing Our Complex Human Nature

Human nature is inherently complex, with its kaleidoscope of emotions, behaviors, and tendencies. On the other hand, this complexity is a richness to be embraced rather than a challenge to overcome.

Our investigation of avoidant attachment was a foray into this complication. It has emphasized the complexities of human emotions and relationships. Understanding and embracing complexity pave the way for a more inclusive, compassionate world.

Recognizing how people perceive, process, and interact with the world promotes a sense of belonging. It shifts the narrative away from alienation and miscommunication and toward unity in diversity.

The Ongoing Journey of Self-Discovery

Self-awareness is a journey rather than a destination. It's an ongoing process marked by epiphanies, introspection, and growth. Our investigation into avoidant attachment has reinforced this sentiment.

Understanding one's attachment patterns has been a step toward greater self-awareness for many. It has revealed new information about behaviors, emotional reactions, and relationship dynamics.

However, this understanding is only the beginning. The journey of self-discovery, with its challenges and rewards, is never-ending. It promises personal development, evolution, and a closer relationship with oneself.

The Power of Resilience and Hope

The twin pillars that support the edifice of human potential are resilience and hope. The importance of these virtues has become clear as we descend into the world of avoidant attachment.

Resilience provides the strength to face challenges, recover from setbacks, and forge ahead in the face of adversity. Hope, on the other hand, illuminates the path. It provides motivation to seek change, hope for a better future, and confidence in one's own ability to grow.

Resilience and hope are invaluable allies for anyone dealing with avoidant tendencies or any other challenge. They serve as the foundation for transformational journeys.

A Final Note of Gratitude and Encouragement

n concluding our exploration, it's imperative to acknowledge the journey. To every reader who has ventured into the intricate realms of avoidant attachment, your quest for understanding and connection is commendable.

The journey has been enriching, marked by revelations, insights, and moments of clarity. It exemplifies the human spirit's unwavering desire for growth, understanding, and connection.

Moving forward, may you harness the tools, insights, and knowledge garnered, forging deeper, more meaningful connections. Remember, the horizon is replete with possibilities, and the potential for growth, transformation, and connection is boundless.

Here's to a future of understanding, connection, and growth, with heartfelt gratitude for your companionship on this journey and unwavering encouragement for the path ahead.

Made in the USA
Coppell, TX
17 January 2024

27788800R00057